THE
PERFECT FICTION

THE

PERFECT FICTION

Gilbert Sorrentino

W · W · NORTON & COMPANY, INC.

New York

ACKNOWLEDGMENTS: *Magazine*, *Wild Dog*, *Promethean*, *Poetry* (*Chicago*), *Fuck You/ A Magazine of the Arts*, *Poems Now* (*Kulchur Press*).

FIRST EDITION

Library of Congress Catalog Card No. 68-14767

Published simultaneously in Canada by
George J. McLeod Limited, Toronto

PRINTED IN THE UNITED STATES OF AMERICA

1 2 3 4 5 6 7 8 9 0

IN MEMORIAM

Ann Marie Sorrentino

1903–1960

THE
PERFECT FICTION

He walks on the street, in
his life. The thunder
gives voice to the heat, a smell

of rain, and trees move.
The alley, cracks, a drain,
peach trees with hard, sour

fruit. The heat itself
a kind of dreadful thunder, trees
crack the sky up into

varied areas
of grey. He is drained, does not
wish to use his voice, one

line of peach sky
holds, in the west. There is
little for him to hold to,

his life, cracked, another
thunderstorm to mark
it: he walks towards home,

a remembrance of clatter,
pots and pans:
and now the rain. He is half

way down the alley, trees
lashed now: "It was late
in the evening when K. arrived."   In snow.

In a fantastic light:
blue of hydrangeas, white
and pink. That light

before the evening starts
to come fast. The sweet smell
of rye and grasses, the

sounds of animals from
the barns, red, of course,
the hand up against

light touching the blossom.
Blue. It must be blue, the
other hand falling

away in casual gesture.
Innocent. The fantastic light.
Caught. Stiff. Concrete.

Where are the rose-colored cities
we dreamed of? Some croaking voice stops
in the head. In the dead

center of the heart. It is one term
of reality: a man stands outlined,
held against the dull grey cities

we have all invented. He pushes
to be seen, and to be understood.
His voice (which is prose) is

all about, not only his voice,
but about the fact that his voice
is prose. The moon is not black,

but might as well be. It is not
visible. The prose goes on, it
makes its own reality, which is:

making a place in what
we dreamed was a place
for a rose-colored

city! The place is
for a voice which
talks about a voice which talks

about its own reality. Its own
term of reality. Where are
the moonlit cities we dreamed of,

and thought of as a possible
entrance to reality? The moon may
as well be black. It is invisible.

Now the night is here. Blood
will stain us, will sustain
us. Nobody's windows have

nothing nowhere behind them
anymore. A stupid face
is part of the pane—don't tell *me!*

Simple, and simply cold, dogs
are barking at the wind. The
lamp shows dirt ground into

the grain of the wood. Wherever
they have corpses, they have maggots:
maggots are only worms, most

of them love rotting lobster
and will feed on men. What wind
is blowing, an old woman who maybe

was kind to her cats is dying
of loneliness. Hers is that face
in the window, how impossibly

remote, how sad to consider it
as part of a pane of window
glass. The part of me I

think of as strength is
black, it is hollow: one goes on,
as one goes on, there is no

explanation. Any stupid bastard
laughs, some can even speak.
That can be a part of happiness.

I own the words I write, the
things I love are mortgaged, my
payments are all partial and erratic.

A particular density: in the center, rises
and forms, making an image. Reality.
A kiss, a strong hand-

shake. A black face moving
out from the paint on either side, drawing
aside

a curtain. A face of unutterable
evil, The Valley of the Shadow
of Death: (he fell

backwards, tripping over
the cans of paint on the floor;
later, he smoked and got drunk.

His head, his brain solid, in
the center, with that black face, now
static, still, frozen peering.

Nothing grimmer than dawn at noon.
It is grey and not awake.
The people are all dead.

All of them too, are dead.
All the people at noon.
These streets with dull sounds.

It is itself. There: and there.
One strikes a foot against the concrete.
One's own foot.

My foot: some of the dead peer at me.
The sun shines beyond this area.
Shining on dead planets.

We do not see it.
Baudelaire was absolutely right.
All dead in this macabre geography.

There is no poetry in me tonight.
Write out of a bitterness: too
many knowing people, wrap

them up: in barbed wire. No
art can assuage their desires, and
they have no human needs

at all. Give them a simple
abstract, say: Red.
Red, Red, Red, Red,

shove it at them. They don't
know what poetry is
so give them Red

to rate. Red, say Red, again.
Say: Fuck you, Fuck you, Fuck
every one of you alike

only my friends, standing outside
this Red I make shall be exempted,
and my friends are who I name.

L the simple shape
a song a baffle for rats
down and up a song

and to the side
a song up and down
and then to the side

L a baffle for rats
to go wrong L the letter
12th in the song

of the alphabet and L
such simple shape a baffle
for rats a tune a jape

In the blue, singa
the song, old corpses
turna to dust, the handa

gone or bones. Old
birds moult or do
something, la la singa

the song. "Man of
destiny," he say, gimme
the smoke, fucka

the world, outa the
blue, singa the song
nothin to do, alla

the people they deada
go wrong, skeletons
no singa no song.

There is "a sound of birds"
which I have never liked. Some birds
awaken others, the world is bird

song, and it is morning.
The same old "light of morning"
in the backyards, a morning

filled with the chance of death:
a man I love has "greeted" Death
again, has felt Death's

"strong hand." My friend
and I have done friends'
duty and have saved our friend

"from himself." Now, over the Bridge.
The sun is painful off the Bridge's
steel: between him and us, another broken bridge.

Gloss On Catullus 58

That the man should be so lost, lost
in time, lost in his love for
a whore. *Nunc in quadriviis et*

angiportis, they were our own
corners. Scotch on the rocks, gin
and orange juice, the same boring

and unassailable sounds of music.
Glubit, to peel the bark from?
"Serves the lusts" says Loeb,

but to peel the bark from
stands out to me, erotic,
"Sucks the pricks" of the

men, standing in that wind,
brothers to those who
are the sons of those who

came over on that well-known
stinking, and "filled with happy
smiles" banana boat. Catullus is dead.

Reality is glass, a glass.
Clarity and a certain bright
reflection. What did he

mean to say? He was reading
some pitiful book he felt
had meaning for him. He was

goaded to some clear anger
which came out words, pointed
with precision, at

his friends: reality, clear
and a glass, reflecting only
itself—not anybody's soul.

Souls are lost, simply, their
value is in what lucidity
they have, reality is never

changed nor tampered with
efficiently, by men. That is
their beloved fiction—if

the moon is paint
in the sky to you, then,
to you, it is paint

in the sky, by God, it
is the moon,
far removed from

all your easy anger, all
the fuming and romantic
fury which you treasure.

There is nothing to solve.
It is: solved equals solved.
The world is proven by identity.

Her voice speaks black
words, they have a shade
of blue, moments pass, or

days, and the words that emerge
are white, the edges are suffused
with yellow, or a pink.

In the still center of time
precise between these colors is
the chuckle of love: it

has no value of color. Its
movement confused with the
plodding of time, but its place

is unique, and still—it is sound.
Two bodies, lost in the blur
of the rainbow, their diversion

far from an art. I watch
them together, pray for the
moment when love breaks

to lust, or lust exists
brilliant and candid. The
rainbow, however, is shading

again toward black, soon words
will enforce it. On the edges
a vague icy blue.

What did he think Hamlet
was? (a huge black man
riding on a motorcycle

was not what he was. Was not,
either, what *he* was)—clipped
speech, his words were

himself? that beautiful man.
Said one thing, and was that
or was that for so long

as he said it (breathing,
so, life stops with its cessation,
so the reality of men, to

themselves, and their beloved
and their enemies):
or was something else,

the language inept to carry
weight: Hamlet is not
Hamlet, is not, certainly,

anything like it, is
some beautiful man who
could not speak, and

who died. Danish rains,
fine, on his grave, no words
for anyone. Is he this

flawed actor who is not
anyone at all? (on the
giant black man's jacket

white adhesive tape
against black leather,
I AM A SPICK.

Something plus something is not one thing.
An insufferable, vicious truth.
One lives with it or one dies. Happy.

Come from the whirling zodiac
"circle of animals"
hoi barbaroi,

if you will, impinge
on this earth, change its
patterns of hate, the love

corrupted and soiled. *Hoi*
barbaroi, the rain of
animals, zodiac fix on

the acts, of us the servants
here of greed and error. Come
from the path of the sun

come, *barbaroi,* pour on
this earth, come, I call
on you. Fix this dirt.

Come all ye Sons of Art
out under the blue, let the
commanders gaze through

their rosy spectacles, one holds
the earth in hand and
the hand gets dirty. Let them

go off in the blue, away, O
Sons of Art, away into
a million Christmas dinners

gallons of egg nog, red
packages and blue to thrill
them (as they will be thrilled

Come away, come away sweet
Sons of Art, the sun that shines
on you is sun clear through.

On the margins of various papers
he draws circles, and lines. They are
suns and moons, what else

could they be? The suns are larger,
their yellow-white light, their
heat, implied by rays

circling their circumference. The
moons are small,
the lonely man in them

realized by careful shading. Outside
it is fast darkening, but these
papers are filled with light!

The suns blaze and rage
in their endless explosions, the moons
are pale and paper-white: all

are absolutely still.
Their systems fully include him, include
as he creates them. What

blistered orb or dead rock
out in space have never meant
to him but in terms

of his own smallness, these
do. These do, he stares through
eleven inches of this mundane gas

at something real. They are
brilliant. They are beautiful,
and absolute: for certain, absolute.

What intense colloquy with the self
will furnish—may be nothing. A
yawn is the reward. This clock,

dull in the room. Confrontation
with a beloved human being is
a superior achievement, is human, is

impossibly difficult. We buy anger
in this time, once in a great while,
a thought is thought. Clear and round,

oranges ripen on a little tree,
across the room, pure in their
orange, the implication of flavor

is intense. The smell of the
blossoms, on occasion, stirs some
fictive and banal nostalgia.

I sit, in my inviolate and
manufactured arrogance, my pen
moves familiarly, the clock,

the night, this light on light
blue lines, the white,
white paper filling with these

words—all at one with
the identical nostalgia, we
are all products of—

"our time"—we call it,
"our" time, as if we ever had
the smallest hold on it.

This disparaging voice—all a
colloquy between two invented
modes, this lonesome mood

which one clings to as a balm,
all some imbecile gesturing at
dignity, and a final barrier to love.

There is no instance that was not love:
at one time
or another. The seasons move

into the past. The seasons shove
one another away, sunshine or rime—
there is no instance that was not love,

one kind or another. Rough
winds at us all now, one kind
or another. The seasons move

away from birds; jays, doves:
or they fly into them, fly, climb,
no instance that was not love.

It is not just some scent on a glove
nor a glittering coin, a dime
or another: the seasons move

unerringly, stolid and bluff.
One would like to find
one instance that was not love;
another;
the seasons
move—

(Sonnet with X's)

Around here's a world that we love:
familiar dullards move
through it. Hello! A groove

in a sky holds sun
which always shines—or shows dun
regardless our wants. Fun

static in *loci* like beaches.
Breasts some men reach
for, soft beneath some wretch's

mouth. There is no winning.
But a constant priming
of the pump, if the timing

is wrong one joins the wrecks.
They merely groan: their spot, an X:
X: X: X: X.

Communications are as love,
confident emotions easily thought positive,
directed toward some Nevada silver

town, filled with ghosts: who
answer!—in a code
the lover only understands.

And sends another message
through the empty air, the
ghosts laugh, the silver

tarnishes, emotions thin
out into formal gesture, empty
as this poem: is construct: artifact:

and the phallus spurts semen
on the ground, the communications
brilliant in efficiency.

What is past is here, as we
will summon it, so dead, but
caught in the mind, sticky

and useless, an old song, half
of the words made up
or hummed. The noble faces

of dead bourgeois who looked
their one time at a hired camera
—some elegance has

shone forth from those
apathetic faces, the camera
is there! to take a picture!

No candid or casual icons
but precise, they exist substantial
in that flesh, those hired clothes.

They have some message
for us, straining we see
dead fashions, white-gloved

hands thrust into pockets,
stylishly—the past thick
concrete between us, heavy

and dark and intransigent,
the X'd window on some
wrecked honeymoon hotel.

Still, it is, as if, one may,
Catch it! Ha.
Ha. Ha. Ha. As in—ha—a pho-

to-
graph: an impeccable scene
from which one smells

honey: honey-
suckle. Play that fucking
thing.

"When I'm takin' sips
from your tasty
lips seems the honey"

suckle Rose. A honeysuckle
Rose, a photographic
pose, a woman so full

of life one weeps
at the death to come
across the lake, to sweep

her up, a spot of
honey. Ha. A spot of love, ho. A
lonely still pho-

to with the smell
of death, over
it, so. So still.

Some hawk-nosed man
striding my old streets,
goodbye forever.

A madman with gold
rimless glasses,
so long pal.

Fat men and lean
that bitter corner,
goodbye, goodbye!

"My youth was a
darkening storm" goodbye,
sweet hearts and pals.

It is one man alone, what
other way
to say it. I am sick of myself.

My loneliness one took
for blazon.
Proud: I am tired of that.

I am a depressing
man, I write
depressing poems.

Alone, sick of myself. Summer
ain't what it
used to be, heart. Of my heart.

How I loved that melody,
a thing, it was, it was
an entity, fresco, substantial,

part of a season, color fixed
in plaster, gentle and mordant
on the air it was. The sound of it

bright over waters of the lake.
Morning. Sunlight. The water
quiet on the raft. My

body, it was, my ear, my
possibility of life, still, a fresco
it was, some melody I forget

what. A tone it was. A mix
of life and time dying
in sunlight: I loved that melody.

The world is still:
in fixed images, stilled:
in my mind.

One drunken night:
bitter Christmases:
lost friends.

Lost—"opportunities":
that pale hand:
raised in the sunlight.

That incredible grace:
that innocence:
that simple gesture.

Still, stilled in the mind:
that grace of innocence:
sunlight, the hand in gesture.

The woman has gone forth
from reality (the world): it is
a doleful place, of course. Going

forth from it is a journey
to one's self—this hegira is said
to be good: even beneficial. You

shake hands with yourself.
She has a kind of adoration
for her crotch, as if it had

a brain, almost as if piss
did not pour forth from it,
several times a day. Likewise

her anus is revered. A garden
of noxious weeds, gripped
by winter, "flowers" in her

free, new soil, her soul.
She has found it! She
has discovered freedom,

it was lying on the ground
all these years, the dead
men, all the intense homosexuals

totally aware of it. God
stinks, she mutters, there is no
God, she says, gripped by

her new reality: her *real*
reality. Her mind
dances through the dying weeds.

❧ ❧ ❧

The stupid painter paints. He
sells his world, or what he thinks
is someone's world. Writers write

their junk, everybody drinks his
booze, is gay, adultery is just another
day in, day out minuet.

Behind this world, is nothing.
This world reveals itself completely—
the painter is a liar, the writer

wants to sell his books and fuck
somebody who says she loves
his work. What strength can I,

who feel these temptations pressing
on my very eyes, draw from these
images of lust, and of success?

It is a total darkness. It is
filled with women who are never
wrong, and when they make some

small mistake, stand in heels
and beautify the whole of day
and evening. God has allowed me

to see only me, and that sight
is enough to drive me to the sources
of a power, any power.

I have love in my hands, all
smeared, red, as in blood or lipstick,
years have deepened the color.

It is the same red that our friend,
the painter, paints. He smiles,
he whistles as he wastes my time.

World is a flame, world
is a–
flame, to him, and to some—

gold fish swim in water, bright
flaming pebbles turned that
from light, paid for and

sun–: world, world, fix
it, make sense, make a sense
from flame. Old Greek

saw it, was right, in his
elemental physics: flow, flowing,
now his physics proved. World

flame, I Sorrentino speak of it
sometimes as flame, most often
as it is: fundamental grey. One

goes on. Read it, read and speak
of it with careful syntax, every thing
battering, falling apart beneath the panes.

What is to be understood:
the world, one's place
in it. The meaning of

it, the meaning of
any part of any of
it, this desk, from

wood, of wood. Quiet
forests underneath the
sky. A blue sky, a black

sky, endless. There is
a pattern, not what we choose
to make, the humiliated artist.

People in Hell are clothed
in coats and dresses, some of
the women wear lace, some

are richer than others, own
a face that possesses white
smiles. In the fashion of that

place, they all say hello
to each other. Such is Hell
in its democracy. Without

the clothes they moan and weep,
that is their fashion, too. This
takes place on Saturdays, after

the parties are through. Over
all, and through the smoke
and flames of the posters

(hung for prospective guests)
absolute horror persists. One
might think it the earth,

but that the evil insists
on being recognized. Dandy
Satan has his choice of pain.

A stinking city full of stinking
people. What things they do
are not flowers, but are sometimes

flowery. They know that they
are garbage and this fact
somehow consoles them. Their

faces grin from the news,
their voices, remembered, are
vomit. But there are flowers

in the sky! one shrieks. There
are flowers in the sky,
agrees another. Hearts pump

blood, long ago sold. These people
are real, are real, they are
absolutely rotten, and are real.

The weight of the rock
on the heart, the earthy
grossness of it, a smell of

turf up, up from one's
depths—the odor of graves.
The hopes that flash in its

surface, dazzling veins
one knows are fool's gold.
No storekeeper, brittle

with greed, will accept it—
each bemused face will marvel
that one's heart keeps pounding.

A heavy heart gives proof
that one lives—let those I despise
float off, their brains grey balloons.

The troops that move in the sun
think they are going to
win. The sun is

utterly white: the wind white
too. The chalky blood
on the wounded simply sets off

the day, a color scheme
for the eye—pain
and death have no tint.

They move, closed in by song,
to where other troops wait,
likewise deceived by the sun.

Here, in the center, a vacuum:
the self. On one side
the glittering crinkle,

spastic, the wondrous
colors of
the flag: over the

police station. On the
other, in a dun-grey sleep
the only color of which

is gold:—money, a bag
of it, as at the end of
the wondrous colors

of a rainbow: so the man
wakes, and dreams, and
wakes. An American.

There is a woman in it always,
for me. And the sea
is glass. In snow and sun-

light, whatever weather one
confronts, the catalyst for each
new season is a woman, for

me. What writer thought
of the mind of God as dwelling
in the sea?—and from there,

controlling. Or was it simply
dwelling, the waves tortuous
and terrifying far above

that brain. A woman
bringing to me the reminder
of the sea, changeless in all

weathers, always in it a
woman, the sea with the
quiet mind of God: I am

unable to say
a word to them, stare,
dumb, they move in nature

to the prodding maybe of
that mind. That writer is dead.
The sea and for me a woman stand.

Take a card, any card
any number, take a Jack
of Hearts. Take the number

six. The number thirty-
nine. 39. A stick
with mud on the end

of it. A hill. Where children
play (the sky somber behind them).
My eyes, 36 years of them.

Brown, color of mud or
a hill, what color does
the other eye of that

one-eyed Jack possess?
(And a sweet sweet chorus
now beginning, hallelujah.

Hallelujah hallelujah
the voices "ring to the sky"
ring out the bold, ring in

the flu, take a number
any number any Jack
has another eye, color of

pasteboard. *Carmen:* if you
don't like my Johnnies
honey, then why

do you dig in my mine?
Thirty-six (it has been proved
is three less than thirty-nine.

For W. C. W.

The black cat is (one might say
silent, a spawn of Satan, those
canny eyes, the glowing

fires in them. The rippling
black fur, black! black! The
muscles sleek, "sheer music"

(or sheer poetry. That uncanny
mind, the head pointed so
to say intelligently, one

might say. O black! O smooth!
O cat, zephyr of evil, black
(one goes on. O soft! O

tense, a kind of music, one
might say a kind of lemons.
(Yellow from the tree.)

Happy
man, he thinks black is
color,

he thinks:
the night is some thing
evil.

For him.
The day is some white
dagger

the sun
in a protestant
fashion

pulls on
the earth which belongs
to him

and night.
Fuck the sun, he says:
the sun

comes out.
Night is my hero:
the night

comes back.
There are no other
comrades.

(*pentagram*)

Who
will
remember

that past
is
past—

beyond
our wish
to

care
for it
?

(the light
frozen
forever:

the night
filled with
water

: rain.
one face
moves us

—
to love
beyond

past—
to
perfect

nostalgia.
One
face.)

Clairvoyant perception of a distant balloon
accident. Clear seeing, clear
eye, clear eye, the far

accident, the yellow or blue
balloon gone in a
P * O * P—a clear-sighted

perception, a clear,
sighted perception. That
distant balloon, that distant

accident. What was yellow
or blue on the clear air
is itself become clear air.

Vivid is the word: of the imagination.
One goes back into the past by its
attendance. Nothing like it

there, where all is vivid, as
imagination. So a constant journey backward
to find the concrete which we thought

we had so well—and *had*, as
imagination, vivid. The dead past
covered over with fresh, with

living flowers brought in hope,
to lend it truth, to render vivid
the hopelessly locked imagination.

My old hat. I never had.
I favor caps—but
my old hat. Comfortable.

Newspapers in the evening. Some
strange man seated in
my chair. The radiators clanking.

A dried-out Xmas tree
with lights and balls
and cardboard Santas. Who

is the man
in my chair? His face
is mine. He has

on my old hat. My old
beloved brown fedora
that I never owned. Creased

in the center as I creased
it. I favor caps. He smiles
at me. The warmth

the comfort of the chair
dragged from the coalbin. Going
back: to that gesture of his

hand: a careless gesture as
he smiles, his hand removes,
he smiles, my beautiful brown hat.

Le beau valet de coeur et la dame de pique
Causent sinistrement de leurs amours défunts.

—BAUDELAIRE

In a dogeared deck of cards
strange lives parallel
our own. Aces, we call

Bullets, three of them
quite enough to kill. The
Queens are Whores—termed

euphemistically, Ladies. Thirty
yards of RR track won't
carry two Johnnys and three

Cowboys: a meld of
elegance and strength makes up
that dazzling House.

The whisper of the shuffle
cloaks the whisper of the Jack
of Heart's pornographic tales,

the cards' lives and fates
alter with each random
deal, each Queen finds

her lover, or is lost
amid a base finance: Kings
murdered by a coalition

of their slaves: Aces
impotent alone. The staring
foppish Jacks

the untrustworthy link
between the powers
and the faceless junta.

Such a long walk to get out
of any pocket, any abstract
                                                    one

Or the real, as read
$$. Or "the blue pocket of the
                                                        night."

Amen. Walk on, walk on, the
cornball old song goes, through
                                                            wind

And so on. Darkness. Rain, out
of the pockets that corrupt us, easy
                                                                  does

It. "The blue pocket" is what
the man said. Lots of smiling faces. Most
                                                                              dead.

A door that opens on
my world, a scene of ice, frozen
crisp, with gin:

a door closes, opens, the eye moves in-
voluntarily across the white
mirage, the harsh bright

fluid posts it, the tongue wants
this balm to move one from the haunt
grim in sunlight: reality.

(A system edged with falsity,
reality is caught winds redolent
of juniper (All the drinkers went

A red sun is going down somewhere
I cannot see it. I have perhaps been there.
Some girl with pimples watches it:

The long blue shadows on the hills.
The trees move imperceptibly, the falls
crack below on boulders, shit

Floats down the river. She is waiting
for her lover, the shadows staining
now her summer dress, she sits

Looking out across the river. A red sun
almost gone, September gone, a red moon
rising and the girl's sweat

Dries. She waits for her lover, black
settles on the earth. One places stock
of sorts in such projection: my pale moon sets.

For M. F.

Inside himself a little song
is singing, he is far away from
old places which are, still are.

Carolina Moon. Still (static), each
thing changing to a new thing,
separate, *El memorioso,* the famous

perro and his famous head.
The liederkranz is still soft
and pungent Max, you do remember

East New York and the home-brew
slivovitz? Smoke goes up to
dusty roofbeams, Xmas lights

are brilliant in it. Carolina
Moon, Mountain Greenery, *O*
what a lovely time it was,

and the grim streets of
el Bronx. Hard city,
harsh and lacking in all

warmth despite its protestation.
The famous dog, Señor Borges,
we have all seen him, O

the endless possibilities, beauty
of calling one year *Carolina Moon.*
Still. Absolutely snapshot.

The perfection of the peg home
the runner flattening out
into his slide, the white ball/painted.

But the light is imagined
is it not? The best kind. An
ordinary light it was, I have made it

something superior, extra-terrestrial.
The flowers of a color ordinary
to them—or a lack of color. White:

everything in the area
of that snapshot that lived
is dead. Gnats, mosquitoes,

flies and worms—those secret
lives all dead as you are
mother. The exquisite

photograph is yellowing,
the edges curled, all those
secret lives are long, long carrion.

Mother, this is a ball of color.
Dazzling, soft, sweet. Could it be
"life"? If one should simply, choose it.

Reach for it. (Don't bother me, go
away, you say, life. Life, bull shit. Life
stops. Abrupt. Sudden. Breath. Out.

The last batter, the long shadows
out across center field, has
struck out looking. K.